Was it a Murder of a Star? or Accident? Of actor Brandon Bruce Lee

Doña Paquita &

Jonathan Brandon Avalos

Doña Paquita

A special dedication in which is a hard job to use free and or spare time to edit, and with her loving son Jonathan Brandon Avalos who cradled the story and helped with his eye for precision, story structure, editing, and taking his time during his own long hours of work. It was something he said was needed to help mom get this book ready for publication.

This book is also dedicated to the memory of Brandon Bruce Lee, the son of martial arts legend Bruce Lee, who died tragically on the set of The Crow in 1993. He was a talented and charismatic actor who had a bright future ahead of him. His death was ruled as an accident, but there are many questions and mysteries surrounding the circumstances of his fatal shooting. This book explores the facts and theories behind his death and tries to find out the truth: was it murder or accident?

"If you see something say something."

In Memorandum

I dedicate this book to Brandon Lee. I mourned him on March 31, 1993. Two years later, my son was born. My son carries Brandon's name, and he says, "It's an honor to carry his name."

Brandon was the son of legendary Bruce Lee, a well-known Martial Artist who died on July 20, 1973, and the son of Linda Lee Cadwell. A memorial service for Brandon Lee was planned on April 4, 1993, at Polly Bergen's house in Beverly Hills, California. Eliza Hutton wore her wedding dress at the service which was poignant (piercing). (P.213) It goes without saying that this death was shocking; it didn't happen because Brandon Lee did something wrong. He only did what he believed was king on the last gun scene in the movie The Crow. Brandon Lee had called his Momzo (mother) Linda Lee Cadwell on the night of his last workday. She stated he was excited talking about his wedding plans with Eliza Hutton. Here is another massive tsunami wave for those who have done wrong to Brandon.

TABLE OF CONTENTS

ACKNOWLEDGEMENTS

I researched information on the following articles in the World Wide Web Budomate "He Shined Brilliantly to Be Remembered."

By Samantha Malagre. James O'barr author The Crow. Inside Edition The Mysterious Death of Brandon Lee. "I wanted to do Mean Streets not Enter the Dragon."-Lee told Empire Magazine in 1992. Brandon Lee on "Hollywood Stunt Makers" Discovery Channel (1991) Linda Lee Cadwell and Shannon Lee. Interviews that Brandon had with the following: Bobbie Wygant Archive 7-13-1992, and interview in which he had which were posted on YouTube, and I transcribed them. R.E. (GUS) Payne; The Death of Brandon Lee: The Untold Story Note from Author: "Brandon Lee was Murdered." The Investigation in 1994 of the death of actor Brandon Lee on the set of The Crow.

Brandon Lee's Last Interview "I don't know if I was destined to play this role, but I feel very fortunate to be doing so."-Brandon Lee

HOW DO I SAY..GOODBYE?

"YOU'RE JUST GOING TO HAVE TO FORGIVE ME FOR THAT." –BRANDON LEE AS
ERIC DRAVEN. Verbatim

ERNIE HUDSON

CO-STAR IN THE CROW

OFFICER ALBRECHT

"SOMEBODY REALLY SCREWED UP. AT SOME POINT, SOMEBODY HAS TO TAKE RESPONSIBILITY, EVEN IF ITS JUST IN THEIR HEART." Ernie Hudson

Ernie Hudson on Brandon Lee and The Crow Remake

"James O'barr who is the creator of it I'm so happy for him yeah and I know it's a business and I wish them well but as far as I'm concerned Brandon Lee was The Crow and he was such a great guy you know I met Brandon maybe about 8 years before we did the movie I was doing a series up in um in Vancouver with Miguel Ferrar they were good friends and Brandon had flown over from uh China where he had been working and um he kind of hung out for about five to six days and I got to know him pretty well so when the crow came up he wanted me to be a part of this film but um Brandon was just one of those rare people you know had a way of in just including everyone you know I mean he was you know some actors and I do it my self sometimes you know you work on set and then when they say cut they go to the dressing room but Brandon was there you know just yeah 100% and um probably one of the life lessons I learned um about I think it was the night before I want to say the night before it might have been two nights but uh my wife's brother passed away unexpectedly um in his sleep un and uh but we were we had to fly from North Carolina to Minneapolis and she was you know upset but we were having dinner with Brandon and at dinner uh he was very nice to hear and then he and I got into a conversation I'm like I've been doing this stuff for so long and I'm like I'm just you know I mean I've done everything I know to do and I'm not getting I was just in one of those spaces and he was saying Ernie hang in he said I'm you know I'm not just starring this I just signed a three-picture deal

9

you know I'm getting married we just bought a house life is good and I'm sure its going to happen for you just hanging there and you be like me you know we flew to Minnesota the next day and as I was walking in the got a phone call that he was dead and I just went wow you know that old saying about if you want to make God laugh telling me plans we don't know it was hard to believe nobody I didn't want to go back and finish the movie but I'm so glad we did because I think he would have been very proud of the movie um his works I amazing and I have no doubt he would have been a major star and he lived but its not for us to know but I really, really love Brandon I think um I see the scene where in the movie where I'm in my shorts with the camp on and at flashback to that night we shot that scene uh it was just hard he was a good guy and it's just breaks my heart that something like that could happen out of carelessness you know just people aren't doing their jobs."

P. 195. The Making of The Crow, Bridget Basse's book. Ernie Hudson had gone to Minnesota, for the funeral of his brother-in-law, and in that already stressed circumstance, learned of Brandon's death just as he and his wife were facing up to personal bereavement: "We heard that Brandon had been shot and that just didn't seem possible. I mean I had done a lot of movies, and nobody really gets hurt, to that extent."

Chapter 1

THE UNSPOKEN

The Key Players—silent, unyielding—escaped prosecution. The laws on gun safety, like fragile threads, snapped. In New York, safety prevailed, but in Wilmington, shadows swallowed the truth. Brandon's legacy flickered, a candle in the wind.

And so, dear reader, we grapple with the unspoken. Was it murder? Was it an Accident? The veil remains. But one truth stands unwavering: awareness is our armor. We honor Brandon by seeking answers, by ensuring safety—for every artist, every dreamer who steps onto a set. May there never be on any stage like a freak circus a…

Fade to black.

I feel that a lot of information was withheld from the public's eye. I believe that some (not all) of the "The Key Players" who committed the crimes were aware of the risk that they had committed and could and did cause bodily harm, and suffering to the innocent at work and as a result it was directly committed against Brandon Bruce Lee on "The Making of The Crow", Bridget Basis authored a book "The Making of The Crow" The Story Behind the Film.

You will get to know the few who were in fact the Key Players who knowingly acted with intent and became indifferent to the risks once a death had been committed but was in fact their actions and choices that led to Brandon's untimely and horrible death. As a result, Brandon Bruce Lee died on the set on the stage and was sacrificed on the set of the Carolco Studios in Wilmington, North Carolina on March 31, 1993. Like it or not that is fact, and it has continued to circulate in the various media sites. Public access.

It's true that property master Daniel Kuttner, stunt coordinator Jeff Imada, and specialist Bruce Merlin dismantled live rounds to create blanks, which is a highly unconventional and dangerous practice. A Cardinal Rule was broken. Additionally, armorer Jim Moyer was sent home on the night of the accident, which has raised questions about accountability and responsibility of the crew members involved. Further, I am asking the readers to *take-into-account* would a life been spared if Moyer had been on set on the last day of the untimely death of actor Brandon Lee? According to Google. More on how Moyer and the Production team failed Brandon.

The secrecy surrounding the events of that night is likely due to a combination of factors, including:

1. Legal and liability concerns: The production company, cast, and crew may have wanted to avoid further scrutiny and potential legal action.

2. Emotional trauma the accident was traumatic for those involved and discussing it publicly may have been too painful for Linda Lee Cadwell. Understandable. In cases when a child is killed the parent is left trying to make decisions that can be traumatic.

3. Industry reputation: The film industry may have wanted to avoid drawing attention to the incident to prevent damage to its reputation.

However, it's important to acknowledge that the secrecy surrounding the accident has also contributed to ongoing speculation, rumors and conspiracy theories. By openly discussing the events and lessons learned, the industry can work towards improving on-set safety and preventing similar tragedies in the future.

With the extensive research that I have compiled and now transcribed into a book for the public to read what was happening during the making of the crow is detrimental to ensure that raising awareness about the onset safety or workplace accidents in general will bring positive result to anyone who works on film, and it should be safe for all involved.

Question: Were the ones who committed crimes aware of the risk that they had committed and could cause bodily harm and suffering to the innocent at work and did they act with intent and became indifferent to the risks. I always felt like closure had not been a part of the answer as to the way Brandon had to die.

I feel that for everyone to get closure the truth must be granted, and it seemed there was a wedge in place keeping the answers locked up. People can lie, people can withhold telling the truth, people can turn the other way and say nothing. I have found that the truth will set you free and I merely wrote what I found and it's what I believe is:

The result of a flawed and negligent system that failed to protect Brandon Bruce Lee from a preventable tragedy. I think that there was a cover-up of the facts and a lack of accountability for those who were responsible for his death. I think that Brandon deserved justice and respect, and not the lies and excuses that were given to his family and fans. I think that Brandon was a victim of a conspiracy that involved greed and corruption. I think that Brandon was more than just an actor. He is now remembered as a real-life hero, a legend, and he continues to be.

Some of the things that the production team did not do for Brandon Lee were:

- They did not hire a licensed and qualified armorer to supervise the firearms on set. Instead, they delegated the responsibility to the prop master Daniel Kuttner, who had no formal training or experience in handling guns. Per Detective Brian Pettus Pg 208.

- They did not inspect the guns before each use and ensured that they were unloaded and safe. They also used real bullets instead of blanks or dummy rounds, which created the risk of a live round being left in the chamber. The duty for Amour was dismissed.

- They did not follow the proper safety procedures and protocols for using firearms on set. They did not clear the area behind the target, they did not keep the gun pointed away from the actors, and they did not have a medic on standby in case of an emergency. Did not follow protocol.

- They did not inform Brandon Lee of the type and caliber of the gun that was used in the fatal scene which was a .44 Caliber Revolver. They also did not let him inspect the gun or rehearse the scene with it. They violated his right to consent and his trust as an actor. By not letting Brandon and Crews members know was deliberately disobeying the laws in place to protect a life and they proceeded to voluntarily meet in secret on the property of Carolco Studios and together held a place between Daniel Kuttner (*Prop Master*), Jeff Imada (*Stunt Coordinator*), and Bruce Merlin (*Special Effects Technician*) P. 202. They were pushing for time according to Pettus. They couldn't stall the scene. They didn't want to spend money on bullets, because they were running behind on bullets. And Bruce Merlin was gonna be a trooper and say, "I can save this money, and I can save us time. Let's just make them!" pg. 206. *That decision in my opinion was criminal negligence and it took the life of an innocent man.*

- They did not cooperate fully with the police investigation and the civil lawsuit filed by Brandon Lee's family. They concealed evidence, destroyed documents, and shifted the blame to others when they entered the crime scene, they looked at the footage and quickly locked it up and evidence without proper consent. (*Tampering with evidence in a crime scene which was brutal and withheld information from the publics eyes.*) They also offered a low settlement amount and refused to admit any liability or negligence. These led to any future suits against the perpetrators. They lived their lives accordingly but did Brandon?

John Gilbert wrote the book "Brandon Lee: The Untold Story Behind His Tragic Death" in 1994, a year after the fatal accident that killed the young actor on the set of "The Crow". According to the book, the production *team did not hire a licensed armorer for the entire duration of the filming.* Jim Moyer was a gun shop owner who provided some of the firearms and blanks for the movie, but he was not on set every day and it has been stated he was not responsible for checking and handling the guns during the scenes. Because he was not hired for the job. He only visited the set occasionally to deliver or pick up the weapons. He also claimed that he was not paid or contracted as an armorer, but only as a supplier. Therefore, he was not the official armorer of the movie, and the production team relied on the *inexperienced prop assistant Daniel Kuttner to load and unload the guns without proper supervision or training.*

The Key Players responsible for his safety and life continue to live their lives to the fullest and continue to deny any wrongdoing after 30 years as, yet I have not read any of the Key Players standing up for Brandon Bruce Lee. Question: *Was there any Loyalty?* Word per word P.205-206.

Pettus believes that the dummy bullets had not been obtained in advance by the prop crew, and now they were needed quickly. He us was never able to get an admission from the production that a completion bond executive actually as in town. That was a kind crossroads in the investigations, because if we could've gotten Grant Hill or Wiley or Pressman or Rosen to say, "Yea, completion bond company was here, yeah, we were over budget and yeah, we were behind time", that would've been a good element as far as criminal proceedings, because then you're gonna rush, and that would be your reason for cutting lines.

But they would never admit there was a completion bond company in town. They would never admit it." Pettus sources would not go on record. He says they were "The guys that know what's going on. The workers, they know what's believe is that the crew was under severe time pressure. Pettus says that he was told by some who were working on the set", that the completion bond company as in Wilmington: "To make sure that its [the movie] gonna be completed on time, it was gonna be completed on budget." Pettus, they didn't want to go on record, because it was their butts if they got caught telling us. Pettus even talked to a local gun dealer about dummy bullets, who told him, "We could've gotten 'em in town overnight for about twenty dollars." [P. 205-206]

In my findings after reading and rereading the book.

Everyone found it easier to *forget* what they did, and it had been investigated and documented that they spoke very little to *save their own skins from criminal charges and be fully prosecuted of the laws in North Carolina.* In all of what has been stated the Laws and regulations on gun safety must be followed through to ensure that all cast and crew members are safe from bodily harm and accidents resulting in death.

The State of New York has had in place for years a great example to follow and keep everyone safe and this way everyone can go home and have dinner with their families and it's something that Brandon no longer had the pleasure of doing. His whole life was taken from him, and he had no choice in the matter. His last call to his loving Mother Linda Lee Cadwell proves the honest and loving son that he was, and she had to carry that with her from the moment she heard her son had been taken forevermore in death.

In my heart I don't believe that justice was served for Brandon Lee, and he was a bright star that shined brightly as stated numerous times. Brandon was an outstanding movie star, and he did not deserve to have his light distinguished. Could he have been a victim of foul play? It's a question many have wondered. It's not easy to try and solve a puzzle that was tossed away after 30 years, and not by his loving family; instead from the ones who let him down.

Brandon's appeal was not only based on his own well-being, but also on the safety and rights of his fellow cast and crew members. He was aware of the dangerous and unethical working conditions that the production company had imposed on them, such as using live ammunition instead of blanks, having faulty electrical equipment, and hiring inexperienced stuntmen. He wanted to protect himself and others from harm, and he also wanted to honor his father's legacy of *fighting for justice and dignity in the film industry*. He was a courageous and compassionate leader who stood up for what he believed in.

Some of the things that Brandon fought for were:

- The safety and rights of his fellow cast and crew members, who were exposed to dangerous and unethical working conditions by the production company.

- The protection of himself and others from harm, as he was aware of the risks of using live ammunition instead of blanks, having faulty electrical equipment, and hiring inexperienced stuntmen.

- The honor of his father's legacy of fighting for justice and dignity in the film industry, as he followed his footsteps of being a martial arts star and a champion of the oppressed and the prejudiced.

- The artistic integrity and quality of his work, as he was passionate about his role in The Crow and wanted to deliver a memorable and meaningful performance.

According to some sources, Brandon Lee did experience dehydration and frostbite while filming the crow movie. The shooting of the film took place in Wilmington, North Carolina, during the winter of 1992-1993. The film had a dark and gloomy atmosphere, which required constant rain machines and artificial lighting. The temperatures were often below freezing, and the actors had to wear wet clothes for long hours. Brandon Lee, who played the lead role of Eric Draven, was especially exposed to these harsh conditions, as he had to perform many stunts and action scenes. He reportedly suffered from dehydration and hypothermia and had to spend time in a heated trailer between takes. He also had frostbite on his fingers, which made it difficult for him to play the guitar for some scenes. Despite these challenges, Brandon Lee was committed to his role and gave his best effort until his tragic death on March 31, 1993.

This lack of proper safety protocols and professional expertise was one of the main factors that led to the fatal accident that killed Brandon Lee. On March 31, 1993, during the filming of a scene where Eric Draven is shot by a gang member, a .44 Magnum revolver was used that had been previously loaded with dummy cartridges by Kuttner. However, unbeknownst to him and the rest of the crew, one of the dummy cartridges had a live primer that caused a bullet to be lodged in the barrel of the gun. When the same gun was later loaded with blanks and fired at Brandon Lee from a distance of about 15 feet, the bullet was propelled out of the barrel with enough force to penetrate his abdomen and spine. (*Other sites have stated it was less than 4 feet when Brandon was shot on the loft by Funboy.*)

He collapsed on the set and was rushed to the hospital, where he underwent several hours of surgery, but died later that day. The incident was ruled as an accidental death by the authorities, but it raised many questions and suspicions about the negligence and irresponsibility of the production team, especially *Moyer, Kuttner*, and director *Alex Proyas*, who were all sued by *Brandon Lee's family for wrongful death.* The lawsuit was settled out of court for an undisclosed amount.

One possible way to prevent such a tragic accident from happening again is to ensure that there are proper safety protocols and professional expertise on the set of any film that involves firearms or other dangerous props. Some of the measures that could have helped keep Brandon Lee safe from harm are:

- Hiring a qualified and experienced weapons expert who can inspect and handle all the firearms used in the film, and make sure that they are loaded with blanks or dummy cartridges that do not contain any live projectiles or primers.

- Having a strict rule that no one except the weapons expert can touch or modify the guns without supervision, and that the guns are always locked and secured when not in use.

- Conducting thorough rehearsals and tests of every scene that involves gunfire, and checking the barrel of every gun before each take to ensure that it is clear of any obstructions or debris.

- Providing adequate protective gear and clothing for the actors and stunt performers who are involved in shooting scenes, such as bulletproof vests, pads, or shields, and ensuring that they are worn correctly and securely.

- Having a sufficient number of trained and certified medics and paramedics on standby, who can provide immediate and adequate medical assistance in case of any injuries or emergencies.

- Following the guidelines and regulations of the Screen Actors Guild (SAG) and the Occupational Safety and Health Administration (OSHA) regarding the use of firearms and pyrotechnics on film sets and obtaining the necessary permits and licenses for such activities.

- Educating and informing the cast and crew about the potential risks and hazards of working with firearms and explosives and establishing a clear and open communication system that allows everyone to report any concerns or problems without fear of retaliation or repercussions.

Brandon spoke on behalf of many when he knew there was something that needed to change so that nobody would be hurt or killed. He was doing exactly what his father Bruce Lee did during his untimely death on earth had done. In which I admired Bruce Lee for what he represented: a fight for the oppressed, prejudices and his son was exactly doing that for others. Then he was the one who died.

I feel I have learned and understood to the best of my knowledge and ability as a human being that Brandon's death was what was an unjustifiable death. Prior to his death, I do believe it was stated it was about 4 days that he had filed against Ed Pressman and Robert Rosen, both producers of The Crow. Brandon did it because of the love for humanity and he had been overworked, and everyone had been pushed beyond the limits. There were not enough breaks and working grueling hours for months because of the pressing time that the movie had to be completed, and it was a non-union and accidents had begun to surface, and many were life threatening.

Co-worker and actor acted as the fictional character Albrecht; Ernie Hudson could not understand why the production would take huge chances in losing their star by putting him at such risk. "It's like killing the goose that laid the golden egg. But you want more eggs! Brandon was in the movie. To take care of him was imperative. How do you not look out for him? And I didn't think they looked out for him very well." (P.132)

Robert Rosen and Ed Pressman denied Brandon's appeal and they dismissed it as quickly as they had received it by Jan McCormack his Manager and Mike Simpson his Agent. In fact, Brandon took the bullet that killed him and stopped him from living his life to the fullest. Justice was not served, and I feel it was an unjustifiable death.

An unjustifiable death is a death that occurs without any valid reason, excuse, or justification. It is a death that could have been prevented or avoided if proper care, precautions, or actions were taken. Example: Guns, ammunition, blanks disclosing important information to Brandon may have stopped him from continuing the last gun-scene.

The result of negligence, recklessness, malpractice, violence; or injustice. Linda Cadwell Lee filed lawsuits against at least 14 entities and won due to negligence. "As a nearly month-long police investigation draws to a close, North Carolina District Attorney Jerry Spivey announces on April 27, 1993, that the death of 28-year-old Brandon Lee on March 31 of that same year during filming of The Crow was due to negligence on the part of the film's crew, not foul play."

Information cited from the article Pop History" Filming of The Crow began in February 1993. Around midnight on the morning of March 31, the cast and crew were filming a scene at Carolco Studios in Wilmington, North Carolina. As Lee entered a room, another actor shot him from 15-20 feet.

Though the gun was supposed to have been loaded with blanks, police later found that a .44 bullet entered Lee's abdomen and lodged in his spine, fatally wounding him. He died in the hospital hours later of internal injuries, blood loss and heart failure. P. 202 *Its stated: "Massee said, "Nobody ever told me not to point the gun at him [Brandon]. And if you watch the film, him getting shot by that gun would be like me pointing my finger across there and shooting you." It was just a freak thing. He was just waving the gun around. Just waving around and pulled the trigger, it was just, randomly, it was an unluck shot." Indeed, it did seem to be the case that while waving the gun around, by an awful chance, Massee had pulled the trigger at the precise instant when it was pointing at the part of Brandon Lee's body where it could do the most damage." word per word.*

As the police investigation began, little was certain about how Lee died, and rumors circulated that the film set was jinxed (there had been a series of accidents), or that his death had been plotted by some unknown enemy.

In the end, the truth was far less sinister, but no less tragic. Hollowed-out cartridges are often used to film close-ups of a gun being loaded; the "dummy" cartridges are then supposed to be removed and replaced with blanks before being fired. The police investigation into Lee's death concluded that a tip of one of the cartridge's bullets broke off from the cartridge and lodged in the gun, then fired at Lee along with the blank.

D.A. Spivey eventually decided against bringing charges against Crowvision, the production company making the movie. Though Lee was to have appeared in nearly all of the scenes left to be shot, the filmmakers completed The Crow using another actor as a double and a good deal of digital technology. The Crow went on to make $50 million at the box office. Close to $100 million worldwide.

An unjustifiable death causes pain and suffering to the victim and their loved ones, and may also raise questions of accountability, responsibility, and compensation. An unjustifiable death is not only a loss of life, but also a violation of human rights and dignity. What had surfaced and was on the news in Wilmington, North Carolina was that before production began, a mysterious caller left a voicemail message warning the crew not to shoot the movie because "bad things would happen."

Question was the voicemail traced or considered? Didn't that ring a bell to anyone? Again, it was Brandon Lee who had filed a formal complaint through his agent Jan MacCormack to the producers of The Crow. Robert Rosen and Edward Pressman were aware of it and did nothing to prevent the death and injuries to the crew members.

The voice message was one of the many signs that something was wrong with the production of The Crow. According to some sources, the caller was a former employee of Crowvision who had been fired and wanted to scare the crew. However, no one took the threat seriously and no investigation was conducted. The caller was never identified or apprehended. The message was dismissed as a prank or a hoax, but it turned out to be a grim prophecy of the tragedy that would soon unfold. Brandon lost his life.

The complaint that Brandon Lee filed was about the unsafe and unprofessional working conditions on the set of The Crow. He had witnessed several accidents and injuries caused by faulty equipment, lack of safety precautions, and inexperienced crew members. He had also suffered from exhaustion, dehydration, and hypothermia due to the long hours and harsh weather. He felt that the producers were cutting corners and putting profits over people's lives. He wanted them to hire more qualified staff, provide better protection, and respect the labor laws. He hoped that his complaint would make a difference and prevent further harm. Unfortunately, his complaint was ignored, and he paid the ultimate price for their negligence.

The effects of exhaustion, dehydration, and hypothermia on the human body are severe and potentially fatal, especially during cold and freezing weather conditions. Exhaustion occurs when the body is unable to sustain its normal functions due to physical or mental fatigue. (over worked 10-14 hours) It can impair concentration, coordination, judgment, and reaction time, as well as increase the risk of injury and illness.

Dehydration occurs when the body loses more water than it takes in, resulting in a fluid imbalance that affects every cell and organ. It can cause headaches, dizziness, confusion, weakness, nausea, and muscle cramps, as well as damage the kidneys, liver, and brain.

Hypothermia occurs when the body's core temperature drops below 35 degrees Celsius (95 degrees Fahrenheit), causing the vital organs to slow down and eventually stop working. It can cause shivering, slurred speech, loss of consciousness, cardiac arrest, and death. These conditions can be exacerbated by exposure to cold and wet environments, such as the ones experienced by the crew members of The Crow.

They had to endure long hours of filming in the rain, snow, and wind, without adequate clothing, shelter, or heating. Brandon Lee had to sit in an ambulance that was warming up to warm his hands, body, and feet, because the producers did not provide any space heaters to keep the crew members warm. This was not only cruel and inhumane, but also dangerous and irresponsible, as it put their health and safety at risk. Brandon Lee deserved better treatment and respect, as did all the other people who worked on The Crow. Co-worker and friend ERNIE HUDSON CO-STAR OFFICER ALBRECHT "SOMEBODY REALLY SCREWED UP. AT

SOME POINT, SOMEBODY HAS TO TAKE RESPONSIBILITY, EVEN IF ITS JUST IN THEIR HEART."

CHAPTER 2

Son of the Dragon
"The Dark Side of The Film".

"Brandon was born on February 1, 1965, at East Oakland Hospital in Oakland, California. He was the son of Martial Artist and actor Bruce Lee and Linda Lee Cadwell. He also left behind little sister Shannon Lee. Brandon learned martial arts from his father Bruce. He was a known martial artist and movie star. "My last name is Lee Bruce Lee " Living between Hong Kong and the US due to his father's career Lee became interested in acting. "JULY 20, 1973, The Well-Known action movie star Bruce Lee's sudden death has shaken" Within days over a thousand mourners crowded the streets of Hong Kong to pay their respect to the fallen super star. Following a memorial service his body was taken to Seattle, Washington where Bruce and Linda had fallen in love. Among those at the funeral were James Colburn and Steve McQueen, who served as pallbearers at the age of only 32. Bruce Lee had left behind a wife and two children. (Brandon and Shannon Lee) and an unrivaled legacy in the world of entertainment and martial arts. Brandon's family moved back to California where Lee began studying with Dan Inosanto, one of his father's students when he was nine Dan Inosanto. Later in his years, he trained with Richard Castillo as well as with Stunt Coordinator Jeff Imada. Lee struggled with his identity having to train in Dojos which had large photos of Bruce lee his father which troubled him. ``

Chapter 3
Dan Inosanto

Bruce Lee was the creator of Jeet Kune Do and taught Filipino-American Grandmaster Dan Inosanto. He trained and was a best friend who earned both trust and respect of Bruce lee. And he kept his philosophy alive for 45 years. After the untimely death of Bruce Lee. Brandon turned to Dan Inosanto and trained well, captivating his audiences from the very first time he was on film. https://www.martialtribes.com/dan-inosanto-on-bruce-lee/ In 1964, according to Martialtribes.com Dan Inosanto handed Bruce Lee his first nunchaku, who thought it "was a worthless piece of junk" Inosanto states that in 3 months, "he was swinging it like he'd been doing it all his lifetime. Further, "without the Yip Man there would never be Bruce Lee and without Bruce Lee there would never be Jeet Kune Do. At times Yip Man didn't want to teach Bruce Lee in front of students. Assigning Willian Cheung and Wong Shun Leung to teach him.

And It Begins

In his early twenties, Brandon became very serious about his acting, and even about martial arts. He returned to the Kali Academy, which had now been renamed The Inosanto Academy. "He was very good as a student here, "Jeff Imada said, "very good as a martial artist. Worked really hard and didn't ask for any special treatment. Some people didn't know who he was. He didn't want to be singled out." Jeff Imada trained with Brandon only occasionally. (P.35-42) Soon Brandon had found a group of guys to work out with. Chad Stahelski was told:

Brandon is going to start working out here, that kind of thing. I was like, "Oh yeah, Bruce's kid. No big deal or anything, but they did want to let us know. I don't know why they were telling us that. Maybe they didn't want anybody taking a crack shot at him or something.

Especially, if he's Bruce's Lee's kid, you've got to be honest with him. But he came in and he was low-key, just a cool guy."

Brandon was already highly skilled in different forms of martial arts and had in fact been certified as a Thai Kick Boxer, passing the difficult tests of stamina and skill. Imada recalls, "He liked to work out and get a little physical and do some strong conditioning and make contact." (P.39-40) Many of Brandon's friends including Chad Stahelski, knew about "The Crow" Comic book! "Someone gave me a copy of "The Crow" just as a birthday present. But I started reading it. This is a pretty bitching comic book! "Me and my buddies used to joke.

After reading the Crow, Brandon was beside himself and wanted to take the chance on becoming the lead man, Eric Draven. He told his manager, Jan McCormack, "you have to get me this part."

"Yeah, what a great movie; that's when we just started doing stunts." Then they got a surprise, when they heard about their friends' next job:

"Oh yeah, Brandon's doing The Crow. And we were all like *so jealous* because what a great movie to work on." As soon as Brandon heard that he might be doing the movie, he excitedly told his friend Jeff Imada about it, saying, "There are a couple things coming up, but one of them I really think is going to be great. It's from a comic book. This guy has got super-human strength, but it'll be different, because the guy can't die." The Crow was offered to Brandon Lee by Bob Rosen.

Brandon had agreed to be working on both: The Crow: The City of Angles & Salvation all by no other than the author James O'barr. Sadly, Brandon never saw his work because of his untimely death on March 31, 1993.

1. The Crow (1994)

2. The Crow: The City of Angles (1996)

3. The Crow: Salvation (2005)

4. The Crow: Wicked Prayer (2005)

29

CHAPTER 4
2-Interviews Verbatim

An interview with Bobbie Wygant Archive 7-13-1992 as follows: "At 17 right out of high school I decided to go hitchhiking, all over the United States had a lot of interesting times. Had some money saved up, didn't spend a lot, my cost was pretty minimal. I had a tent in a tent I camped out."

"Was that a time when you just wanted to find yourself and find where you wanted to go, what you wanted to do?"

"Yeah, I suppose so. I was probably trying to replicate some of the books I had read while I was growing up on the road or whatever."

"And your mom was back in California, and you stayed in touch or not?" "Yeah, I'd call her from a payphone every once in a while, you know say, I'm fine. I'm alive, I'm still alive. I haven't been washed away by the rain or anything like that, this was the year the time out in California that the really bad rainy season came and all of Malibu the Malibu Coastline just got washed away. And I remember hitchhiking all the way to the coast highway and the devastation of everything was gone. It was interesting. I made my way all the way to the Zen Monastery called Tassajara near Big Sur and spent a little time there. It was interesting."

"Did you observe that philosophy and practice it or...? "No, it influenced me a little bit, but I certainly didn't join up and shave my head."

"Then you came back home and then what?"

"Came back home, got a job working at a restaurant for a while and took the GED the high school equivalency exam and went to college for almost a year, dropped out of college got a job working for a producer, did some auditions got my first acting job and been doing it ever since."

"What was your very first acting job?"

"First one I ever got paid to get my Screen Actors Guild Card for was this TV movie called Kung Fu the Movie. And it was a spinoff of that venerable old series with David Carridean, and I played his long-lost son in it."

"Now did you do any martial arts in that?"

"A little bit yeah, but nothing like Rapid Fire, we were a little hampered by television morality, you know?"

"When did you learn or how did you learn the martial arts?"

"I started learning martial arts with my dad."

"Oh really?"

"Right about as soon as I could walk that was really kind of like how we played at my house, you know and my dad was always training a real fanatical trainer very dedicated to his art, and so he always had students over in the back yard working out and I'd always be out there imitating them and then eventually my father started training me pretty seriously. Um and after he passed away there was a couple of years that I didn't work out at all, which was during that time that I was talking about before when we first moved to the United States, and then I took up training again when I was about 13 with the man who is still my sifu today a man named Danny Innosanto who was my dad's senior student at the time of his death so it's kind of a nice line a broken line."

"When did you make the first movie when you were the star?"

"First thing I ever did that I had a starring role was this film in Hong Kong called "Legacy of Rage"

"Did we see it here in the states?"

"Not unless you speak Cantonese no, it's a Cantonese language picture, so obviously it didn't play in America, it played in ChinaTown and stuff in New York and Los Angeles. And it was fun a lot of fun it was very interesting in an Asian production company they do things differently they don't have the guilds that we have in the United States Screen Actors Guilds and all the different unions and such and so everything's a lot more like from what I understand from my reading that Hollywood used to be in the twenties it was more like "you grab the light and you grab the camera…and what shall we shoot today?" We just kind of made it up and improvised it and at the time it was nerve wrecking, but it was actually a good experience.

"And were you the star?"

"I was the star."

"Okay. And then the second movie then?"

"I did "Show Down in Little Tokyo" last year in which I was co-starring with Dolph Lundgren and that film I didn't have a lot of input into. It was really just a job for me, but it was a good experience too. Rapid Fire was the first time I ever starred in an American Motion Picture and I had a chance to do the fight choreography for the film too along with Jeff Imada the Stunt Coordinator and so it was a lot of responsibility you know so it's really my first big shot I guess you can say."

"Brandon, did you initiate the project or did they come to you or what?"

32

"I managed to be using that footage from the film that I had done in the east I managed to get myself into a situation to make a movie with 20th Century Fox and then the movie was actually developed for me so that was really nice because I had a lot of input into the form that this movie eventually took."

"The movie..I just came from the film, and it is nonstop action I mean is just boom, boom, boom you know it never lets up. But a lot of people may think it's all just martial arts, but it actually incorporates a lot of different kinds of action."

"Yeah, when you make a martial arts movie in the modern world you're faced with the problems of guns. (Brans contagious laughter) You know? I mean the simple fact of the matter is if anybody has a gun, there out of range you're in big trouble you know. And as a choreographer in the film, I wanted to address the issue whenever there was a gun in the room because sometimes it's very convenient why doesn't someone just pull out a gun and shoot him you known, and um and we had some people some in the movie and some who were from the opponents are from the Italian mafia, we assume they were not martial artist they were more like street fighting and the other group of bad guys were from Asian gangs so we figured they would have some martial arts skill so we got a chance to mix it up a lot to do a lot of different things ."

"The very opening scenes of the film that I found fascinating, where was it filmed at?"

"It was in Thailand."

"It just had to be on location, you know it just had to be."

"It was on the River in Thailand."

"For people who are into martial arts, what are the different kinds of martial arts represented in this film?"

"My training lies in "Jeet Kune do" which is the art my father created while he was alive, in the film you'll see influences of that there's also some Thai kick boxing in there and there's a little bit of Filipino eskrema which is the stick stuff you'll see in the film, there's some American boxing in there, my father's art of "Jeet Kune do" he took the best from the arts that he had studied and he compiled it along with what he added himself into this art that he called Jeet Kune Do which is known as "the way of the intercepting fist "and he really pioneered what came to be known and is known today as the "ecliptic martial arts" means you draw from different sources you know so there's actually a quit a great deal of stuff in the film it's all stuff that I that very comfortable doing its all techniques stuff that you use although admittingly the fights as they appear in the movie are not my idea in the movie how a real fight would happen their sensationalized their theatricalized to a point you know but that's due to the nature of this film at a later date I would interested in doing a film where the martial arts are portrayed in a realistic fashion as I think that might be pretty interesting."

"You did shoot in a location in Chicago."

"Mmhmm."

"And did you actually shoot the location stuff at the L on the tracks or was that L rigged up Hollywood stuff?"

"Yeah we did it was right in the middle of summer and just about year ago this month or next month actually almost a year ago and it was hot and a we were shooting nights up on these elevated train tracks and there's that third rail you know the electrified rail that the train runs on and if you touch it when it's on your dead right and the thing of course the power is off while we wore working but you know you just imagine some guy sitting in central going why is this switch off let me see (switch off noise. lol) And it was a very treacherous place to work. There was all these gaps when the boards and it was about thirty feet below and it was hot, and it was the end of the shoot and it's all action you know but it was fun. I liked Chicago a lot."

"Did you at any time use a stunt double?"

"Yeah, sure there's some going through a plate glass window, you know that's not me. I do all my own fighting because that's just part of the bag you know I mean it's part of why I am up on that film and I wouldn't want someone else to represent me my style in the film but stuff like going through a plate glass window or a getting thrown into a bar full of glass bottles Yeah I had a great stunt double named Jeff Cadiente. I've learned as I've gotten a little older that it just doesn't do anyone any good for you to get hurt on film because it just slows everything down, it costs everybody a lot of money and it puts a lot of people out of work. You know it's not a particularly responsible thing to do."

"What was the budget on this picture?"

"It was about 15 million. Dwight Little he is a hot shot you'll be hearing of him."

"Is this his first?"

"Not at all he did "Mark for Death, with Steven Seagal", and he did one of the Halloween pictures and I'm sure he has done some other things that are not as well known."

"Do you have another picture you'll be coming out?"

"I have another picture I'm just getting ready to start working on called "The Crow" and I'm really excited about it.

"What is that?"

"It's a supernatural piece about a rock musician and his girlfriend who are murdered, and he comes back from the dead to revenge his own murder and the murder of the woman that he loved and it's quite interesting and it's very dark and very surrealistic."

"Who else is in it?

"No one yet."

"Oh"

It's just me so far."

"Yeah, okay alright Brandon, you're a very articulate charming young man and I really enjoyed our time and congratulations on Rapid Fire."

"You're welcome. It was a pleasure."

Brandon Lee on Hollywood Stunt Maker Discovery Channel (1991)

Interview-2 Verbatim

"Showdown in Little Tokyo"

Brandon Lee words: "YOU KNOW"

"The martial arts genre is special to me because it's always been more interesting in my opinion to watch two men who are possessed of skills in the martial arts fights with each other than to watch people shoot at each other because as my father said in "Enter the Dragon", "any damn fool can pull a trigger." For me the most exciting thing in the martial arts is the choreography itself (*you know*) it's really wonderfully created to be able to choreograph a fight scene (*you know*) on this film "Showdown in Little Tokyo" a choreographer name is Pat Johnson who is wonderful it's been great to work with him and a on the next film I expect to have a little more of it on my own shoulders and I am looking forward to that much it's wonderful and (*you know*) and you think it out and after all the training you had in martial arts academy's you've come to realize those certain golden moments that happen in a fight when it's just perfect (*you know*) when it's just perfect and the guy steps right into it and there's nothing like it in the world and so you can create those you can make it happen that each tie and its great. I think the thing that is special to my father's impact is that he really created a genre where there wasn't one. "The Return of the Dragon " was really interesting is that my father wrote it, directed it, and started it. It was Chuck's first acting role I believe and the fight scene in the end that between Chuck and my father is the finest film that I have ever seen one to one on film. There are so many nice little things in that film that shows it's a fight between two fighters (*you know*) what I mean little things I mean real little things (sound effects mimicking) I was 8 and a half when my father died and he was 32 we lived in Hong Kong at the time so upon my father's death we moved to

America my mother my sister and I it was just a real different thing a whole different school system different culture standards I mean everything was different (*you know*) and we went from living in a large house where I remember every day when we'd go to the school they would open the gates and have to push people out of the way for us to (*you know*) get the car out to be able to the school we went from that to living in relative security in America which was a blessing it really was great (*you know*) and I have my mother to thank for that but a it's a lot of things changed I just believe that my father would want the achievements of his life which were great lasting until this 18 years after his death (*you know*) he would want me to have and I'm really grateful to that (*you know*). I know that he would not want me to attempt to become "a pale carbon copy of himself" I believe that and besides I don't have no desire to, and I couldn't anyway (*you know)* I'm another person and hopefully I'll have my own book to write."

He was outstanding as an actor and as a human being he had a lot of passion for life. With his rebellious attitude it stemmed from the loss of a father, a mentor, a teacher and a best friend as he fought hard trying to be his own person, whilst living in the shadow of his famous father who was a Legendary and famous Bruce Lee a Martial Artist known worldwide was hard to gain his own identity and make his own path his way. After a few popular action films, Brandon was signed to a few studios including 20th Century Fox and Carolco for three-picture deals.

CHAPTER 5
THE RAVENS

The Crows the making of the crow exclusive interviews Mirmax (Verbatim)

"The Crow in the film, the bird in the film, you could really just look at as a guide almost a piece of his own personality that guides him back into his life and reminds him who he was what happened to him, this is a person who has been pushed right to the limits of his ability to cope of what is going on and in a sense is quite mad sometimes, in a sense is completely insane almost in a sense that you might think of a insane person having voices, you know, more rational voices that try and guide him, more irrational voices that come from a more emotional a more deep seated place I think that the crow is that rational voice…the crow is his guide the crow helps Eric do what he has to do in a very practical sense it leads him it to the places that he has to be it helps him find the people that he has to find, it's a story about justice for victims (each one of these is a life the life you helped destroy) his mission is to find the men who killed him and his fiancée and kill them (Gentlemen, I just want him) it's a wonderful role and it really is a role that you have to take risk with it gives you a wonderful opportunity and take those risk and stretch because you tell me how somebody who comes back from the dead is gonna behave you know,

(If you move your dead, and I say I'm dead and I move.) and that's one of the wonderful about playing this character it's a real..you can really take the gloves off in playing this part because there are no rules about how a person who comes back from the dead is gonna behave who (listen I'm sure you'll remember you killed them on Halloween, it can't be you, we put you through the window there ain't no coming back) and there it the part of him that is filled with rage, towards what was done to him, and one of the things I like best about this movie is the fact is that all of those parts of the characters are given balance on the screen, he's torn up, he's torn up really badly, emotionally, physically and psychically (she uh, died at the hospital, don't touch me, I saw her through your eyes). I think that the appeal of Eric's mission is that it is a very pure one, he has come back to seek justice, (knife scene).

I've done other films that have had a violence, in them but I must say I never done anything where I felt that the violence wasn't as justified as it is with this one, there's very little need to worry about compassion (victims aren't we all) this is justice you know and I truly feel that it is and I truly feel that If I was on the same situation I would do the same thing he has something to do and he's forced to put his pain long enough (tell them death is coming for them tonight) this film deals with a balance between good and evil (I gave this to shelly once I think she'd like you to have it)

I believe what Brandon was expressing was that the CROW is his link to the living world, his only companion in his lonely quest. The crow is also a symbol of rebirth, of transformation, of resurrection.

The crow represents the power of love that transcends death and brings Eric back to life. The crow is both a protector and a witness, a guardian and a messenger.

The crow is the soul of Eric, the essence of his being, the voice of his conscience. The crow is the key to understanding the character of Eric Draven, the hero of The Crow."

In all I feel that Brandon did something wonderful in his acting as he brought Eric Draven to life with his creativity and beautiful acting and demonstrated how a person would act if they were allowed to return from death and right the wrong of what the film strongly brings out in O'barr writings of a real Crow in the movie it truly is magnificent work.

CHAPTER 6
The Making of the Crow

On March 31, 1993, Brandon Lee-stood on the set of "The Crow". He was about to film a pivotal scene-one where his character, Eric Draven, would meet his demise. But life mirrored art in eerie ways. As Brandon prepared for the role, fate had other plans. It bit a hole in everyone who loved and adored him as a son, brother, uncle, cousin, friend, fiancé, actor and human being.

In a tragic twist, a prop gun fired, and a dummy bullet struck Brandon. The scene meant to depict Eric's death became Brandon's own. Six hours later the 28-year-old actor was dead. The crew had already sensed a curse-a carpenter nearly electrocuted, a sculptor crashing a car. But nothing could prepare them for his loss.

Ironically, just days earlier it was Brandon who had taken his time to ensure that nobody would continue to get hurt due to negligence or penny-pinching individuals as he had filed with Jan McCormack his agent to no avail as Ed Pressman *Producer* of the movie with Bob Rosen *Executive Producer* refused and or rejected his appeal. The result could never be erased from what was about to happen and did happen in real life of a star who shined brightly.

In the Make-up trailer, Lance Anderson, as routine, did Brandon's make-up. Lance began first by adding a light base on his face it was all that was needed on his natural complexion, because on this particular scene, Brandon was going to be Eric Draven the fictional character for the movie he was excited in being a part of and he even stated on an interview speaking from his heart, ***"I don't know if I was destined to play this role, but I feel very fortunate to be doing so."***
-Brandon Lee

Brandon's hair was different, not like the usual wet down long hair, rocker wild look on stage but instead it was a perfectly brushed look. Michelle Johnson is his Make-Up Artist and she stated that for the very first time she didn't have to add any hair extensions because his hair was the right length to his shoulders. She considered it odd. (Verbatim.)

"The Crow started principal filming on February 1, 1993, Brandon's 28th birthday. The painstaking schedule on The Crow was beginning to take its toll on Brandon as he was working on overload into *19 hours straight, when fatigue kicked in the hardest and pushed insomnia to a point of being an overload coming from a lack of sleep and it's when depression conditions on set actually allowed Brandon to take a closer look at what he pegged "SUBHUMAN"* conditions as the cast and crew were being forced to work at any cost.

It's fact, due to the hideous working days and nights just like slaves in which Brandon himself stated were all *"subhuman"* and it's why he took it upon himself with his agent to file complaints against such horrific labor laws that had been denied by Producer Ed Pressman, and Bob Rosen Executive Producer handpicked by Ed Pressman himself.

More accidents were beginning to surface and even after the much-stated near death to one of the carpenters Jim Martishius, got electrocuted, while on the back lot, high up on a cherry picker, accidentally backed himself into live power cables. In the production office, *Greg Gale* noticed, A little flinch in the power, and we heard about five minutes later that there had been an accident. ``

The miracle was that Jim Martishius, in contact with thirty thousand volts, was not immediately killed. Yet, his clothing was in a blaze. (P.83) And Martishius was trapped in the cherry picker's cage. He was 6 ft. two. It took 2-3 minutes to get to him and to the ground. He was already engulfed in flames.

Martishius was very badly injured, and we didn't think he was going to pull through, recalls Greg Gale. Everybody thought he was going to die. He had second and third degree burns over eighty percent of his body, but eventually he went back to work at the studio. (P.84) He lost both ears. Made jokes about it himself. Legal issues rolled in for Crowvision.

It wasn't long before the penning pinching oversights on the $14 million production started to be plagued by mishaps; a stuntman accidentally fell through a roof breaking several ribs, and an unexplained fire almost destroyed one of the backlots. It had already been a hard two months of working overtime from twelve to fourteen-hour days.

Per the same report, On Saturday March 28, 1993, four days before he died, Brandon lodged a formal complaint to his agent, Mike Simpson and manager, Jan McCormack, which was sent to Executive Producer, Bob Rosen. Rosen's response was less than comforting. McCormack last words to Rosen became prophetic, "you guys are killing Brandon down there."

Working extra hours on film sets is not unusual, says Mike Simpson, Lee's then agent at the influential William Morris Agency, but even he found this excessive when he visited the set several weeks into production.

Actors are meant to get a certain amount of downtime between rapping one scene and starting the next. There are provisions for violating that, you pay a fine, which is called a force call payment. But there can also be a limit on how many forced calls per week you can have, and they were violating it, cutting corners, "explains Mike Simpson.

And because of the accidents that escalated Brandon took it upon himself for the safety of others to try to get the labor hours required to be readjusted to allow the crew of "The Crow" to rest as every other human ought to be.

Of course, late Ed Pressman Producer was not happy about it and said profanities and denied it. According to what was being said it was all about the money and already being behind and Executive Producer Bob Rosen & Producer Ed Pressman were not going to budge.

A full-blown investigation by the North Carolina OHSD, Occupational Health and Safety Division followed (a mere $9,500 fine). In what was an unrelated fire on the first night of The Crow, a brand-new equipment truck belonging to the Key Grip Chunky Huse was engulfed by flames.

Production Manager, Grant Hill named the new job to Clyde Baisey as Safety Co-Coordinator on the film; not a certified paper supporting him being in fact a medic has surfaced according to the book "The Making of the Crow," by Bridget Baiss, has not been stated.

At some point a crew member, without giving it much thought to safety, had put a blanket over the door to keep out the cold. And because it had been forgotten a light bulb that was mounted on the door and ignited it, as you can imagine smoke and fire damaged the interior of the new truck belonging to Key Grip Chunky Huse.

Strangely, during the shooting of The Crow, Hudson was never aware of Clyde Baisey's heated ambulance in which Brandon sometimes sheltered. At any rate, Hudson was certain that, "if he had not demanded the production provide heater on the back lot we would have done the whole movie in the cold." (P.131)

All through his first night on The Crow, the thing occupying Ernie Hudson's mind was that he was extremely cold. "I got there; I was freezing. And I asked where the heaters were. They had no heaters, and I was going lie, wait a minute here!"

Hudson had worked in uncomfortable conditions on many movie sets, but this time, he was totally shocked!" "The little girl was there with her little summer outfit, and they didn't dress for winter. She was freezing and there was no place to warm up and I thought, man, this is ridiculous.

And they told me, "Well Brandon's been walking around in bare feet and no shirt on, and he hasn't complained. But I thought, naw, naw."

During the shooting of The Crow, it was shot in zero temperatures so cold that the warm water in the huge sprayers to simulate rain would freeze before hitting the floor. In fact, they had to add alcohol to the water to prevent it from freezing.

And keep in mind that Brandon was filming during the freezing temperatures without a shirt, shoes, and jacket. There are plenty of photos that Robert Zuckerman the still Photographer took during the making of The Crow.

Grant Hill, the Production Manager, at that point decided to ask Clyde Baisey to be the Safety Co-Coordinator on the film. Baisey suspected that this newly created job could be merely a way from the production to protect itself against future penalties. "I'd be the heat man for it, right", he says. It'd take the monkey off their back and put it on mine. And I told him, no! I wasn't interested in doing that. I'll just be the medic." Verbatim. (P.85)

Continued: As the medic, Baisey's position didn't carry the responsibility of overseeing and enforcing all safety precautions; perhaps the most important part of his job was: The Co-Ordination of all EMS, [Emergency Medical Services] on the film." If an accident happened, he would provide immediate, basic medical attention while the local paramedics were on route. Nobody could have imagined what a crucial task this would later turn out to be. Verbatim. (P.85)

CHAPTER 7
Dismantled Bullets

Why was that stated in investigations by Payne? It is also possible that a live round .44 Magnum bullet was left in the weapon after it had been fired that evening by an 'extra' on the backlot of Carolco Studios. Because. The Prop Master Daniel Kuttner, Stunt Coordinator Jeff Imada, and Specialist Bruce Merlin all dismantled the back of Daniel Kutner's pickup truck and did in fact dismantle the live ammunition on the backlot. Question: Who bought and took the live bullets to the Prop set?

Set Dresser, Marthe Pineau. Along with a handful of others walked into the Pawn Shop and purchased the items which included the live box of ammunition .44 caliber bullets and which Pineau believed to be dummy bullets. Who brought the live bullets to the set without noticing they were not dummy bullets? Did she have permission to buy the ammo? It's never noted. Question? Is it because she didn't know they were real live bullets, and here she purchased them believing they were blanks! (P. 205).

Question: At what point from her purchasing them did the salesman on the counter of the Pawn Shop look at the bullets and realize they were either dummy bullets or live ammo? Investigations do not draw a clear picture. Was the buyer questioned at the pawn shop? Did she have a license to purchase live bullets? And what was the name of this pawn shop in Wilmington, North Carolina where this purchase took place? (See video on "Unsolved Mysteries Part 1 & 2" on Bruce & Brandon's mysterious death for the answer.) Do you as the reader want to know the answer? Here it is, it wasn't stated in the Unsolved Mysteries Part 1.

Who brought the gun (.44 Caliber) into the set on that day? Answer: The Property Assistant, Charlene Hamer, had got the gun from the prop truck belonging to Daniel Kuttner, parked outside the stage. Did Charlene Hamer have any knowledge of handling firearms? Was it questioned by the investigators? Did anyone get charged with selling, handling and discharging a gun at any time while the Crow was filming?

The Book states that there were certain individuals that did indeed practice shooting the .44 Magnum a few weeks short of the filming (the last gun scene with Brandon the star) of The Crow. Pettus now had to discover where the gun had been before the fatal shot, and when it had last been used.

Daniel Kuttner told Pettus that: The gun had been secure in his truck since the Second Unit had used it for filming. That was a surprise to us. Number one, they never told us anyone had used a gun. As far as we knew, that [the scene when Brandon was shot] is the first time this gun had been used. See? P.203.

Which was in fact Michael Massee (Funboy) and Daniel Kuttner (Special Effects Technician). Not Brandon (Eric Draven)

A huge Cardinal Rule had been broken. It was later stated that a box of blanks would have cost $20 bucks, (P.206) (Kuttner, Merlin, Imada) and perhaps it may have taken a day to arrive, it would have been a reasonable amount of money. Brandon would have not been killed. Investigator Pettus even talked to a local dealer about dummy bullets, who told him, "We could've gotten 'em in town overnight for about twenty dollars."

The whole unfortunate thing is that the dummy bullets became an easy fix for Kuttner just because he states that Bruce Merlin's experience as a Special Effects Technician did qualify him to make the dummy bullets from the real ones. Detective Brian Pettus stated in his report that it was documented that neither *Kuttner nor Hamer* had *any* experience with guns and Kuttner did not have *knowledge about the gun that he loaded and handed to Michael Massee.* See?

So, knowing they needed dummies for the bullet-swallowing scene, Bruce Merlin told Pettus that he said: "We can make some." So, they went back and made the dummy bullets, in the back of Kuttner's truck. While they're doing this, [Merlin says] "You're gonna need some full load blanks, so just go ahead and make those too. Kuttner says, "You know, I'm real uneasy about this whole thing."

Kuttner was uneasy because what they were doing was pulling the bullet apart with pliers, emptying out the explosive powder and then detonating the primer. Pettus says, "They didn't have the proper tools. All they had was a pair of pliers. And they pull them out, just like you pull a tooth out."

Daniel Kuttner, Property Master, Stunt Coordinator Jeff Imada and Special Effects man Bruce Merlin, removed the gun powder, crimped together the bullets. But the men had failed to fire all the primers (which is the charge of a bullet) when they used the rounds for filming. One primer had not discharged properly leaving a piece of the lead tip of the bullet with a primer in the barrel of the weapon.

When the gun was needed for the fatal scene, it was re-loaded with blanks (which are harmless show bullets without any charge), causing a lethal charge that had the force of a real .44 bullet. "Mike Simson stated that it was worse than one bullet; it was like two bullets firing out at the same time." The book makes note of the fact of rumors had surfaced of some crew members had been using drugs while filming of The Crow.

Why was Jim Moyer not around to ensure the safety of the weapon a .44 Revolver had been followed through? Who sent him home early?"

This raises a serious question about the *competence and negligence* of the crew members who were responsible for handling the guns on the set. How could they entrust such a crucial task to someone who had no expertise or training in firearms?

Why did they not follow the proper safety protocols and check the revolver before handing it to Massee? Clearly, if Moyer had discovered the blank, he would have used his professional knowledge and used precautions during the few minutes prior to allowing Massee to handle the gun and be using it.

What if there was a live round mixed with the dummy rounds, or a fragment of metal lodged in the barrel? These scenarios could have been easily avoided if Moyer was present and inspected the guns as he normally did. Question: was it Moyer who was hired, had he been hired? Was he just helping or filing in. Whose job description was the one hired to keep the gun safety at play to ensure nobody was hurt during the film making process.

"Detective Pettus had talked to Assistant District Attorney, John Carricker, who had sent the fatal bullet over to the State Bureau of Investigations Department in Raleigh. They came back with some very interesting information about Carricker. They found black powder. That's right. Its significance is—its black powder. The only way black powder could have been on the back of the bullet was, black powder fired the bullet out.

The only way black powder could've fired the bullet out is-if they had a blank in there."
Black powder is used in blanks, instead of the usual explosive, because it produces a flash flame
from the end of the barrel, which movie goers like to see.

Daniel Kuttner told Pettus that: "The gun had been 'secure' in his truck since the Second
Unit had used it for filming. That was a surprise to us. Number one, they never told us anyone
had used the gun. As far as we knew this [the scene when Brandon was shot] is the first time this
gun had been used." See?

Pettus had to wonder if they were being deliberately obstructive. "You had a lot of
people." he decided, "who were scourging around trying to salvage their careers. They've been
attached to this movie, and they had many mishaps, and now there's a death. They were trying to
distant themselves from it." (P.203)

But instead, Moyer was sent home, and the crew decided to cut corners and gamble with
Brandon's life by allowing someone who knew nothing about weapons and had in fact told Pettus
he didn't have any knowledge about weapons he was just doing his job offered to him to do. And
they lost. Brandon Lee was sent home in a compartment and would be laid to rest next to his
father Bruce Lee in the state of Washington.

According to R. E Payne he stated:
Jim Moyer, the expert weapons handler, had been sent home and wasn't on the set; there wasn't
really anyone qualified to check the weapons correctly. So, the theory developed that what
happened was an accident, according to investigating officers. *"It was never investigated to
where that kind of result was ever possible."*

CHAPTER 8
And NO VEST

Sofia Shinas, Shelly Webster character stated, however, is sure that when she went to the set that night it was news to her that she was going to be shot. She thought she was simply going to be raped and beaten to death[!]. Arianne Phillips also remembers that it was decided on the night that Shinas *"was going to get shot"*. Who then would get shot, was it *Shinas or Brandon*? And it was being *juggled around who was going to be wearing the bulletproof vest either Brandon or Sofia Shinas.*

According to the book by Bridget Basis it was Sofia who questioned Director Alex Proyas and was upset because she was being pulled to the left and to the right with the whole scenario and she was very uncomfortable about it. Something went wrong, something nobody knew was coming. Did Brandon get to look and read the script change from a knife scene to a gun scene? Well, Brandon Lee isn't here so I can't ask him. Does anyone know? I didn't read any notes on what was happening.

Sofia Shinas spoke about it happening to her. It's not noted in the book *"The Making of The Crow"*. When investigated why was it not noted about the script change. I'm yet to read it on any of the investigations by the Wilmington Police Department. Was it questioned? Sofia Shinas stated, *"Alex Proyas changed his mind twice about how Eric Draven and Shelly Webster were to lose their lives."* At first, Proyas decided that Shinas would be shot. She then put on her bullet-proof vest. Oh my! Jeff Most said that: "The next day Sofia Shinas related to me that, while she was in Make-Up, getting final touches, the Wardrobe Supervisor Darryl Levine came in and said, Well, Alex's gone back to the original shot, I need the suit vest, and the amour protection to be taken off it, to be given to Brandon."

Who said in front of Shinas, that he was not going to put the vest on. He didn't want it to be seen in the shot. "The Wardrobe Supervisor Darryl Levine showed him it wouldn't be, but Brandon said, "I'm not going to put it on. If it's my time to go, it's my time to go." And he went on and did the scene without the armament vest on. What? No, Vest on Set?

It had further been stated that Sofia Shinas would wear the bullet proof vest and shield, to its being in her possession in the wardrobe room to it being changed and it being Brandon who would be shot, and the vest was available to him on that night."

Part of the original safety plans for the production had involved Brandon wearing a bullet-proof vest for scenes which needed it, such as the big shoot out in Top Dollar's boardroom. But nobody thought that the action in the scene they were about to shoot in the loft merited that kind of protection. *Jeff Imada believed that: "It was very safe. Normal squibs. There was no need for him (Brandon) to wear a vest that night, really?"*

When asked on an interview here is what Brandon stated about wearing a bullet proof vest: "Well, it means I'm wearing a bullet proof vest. I never got shot 20 times by squibs before and it's an experience everyone should have. It's a NAR Day; No Action Required Day". – Brandon Lee-

Perhaps *there was rhyme nor reason for him to say he wouldn't wear one* and just maybe it was not available to him the night of the gun scene between him and Funboy character aka Michael Massee on that fatal night. Because it was a last-minute change by Alex Proyas, said Director of The Crow, it could have been the vest was not available to him and yet, with all the confusion on who was going to be shot and who was going to be wearing the bullet proof vest and he didn't wear one. Yet, recall it was Darryl Levin who took the vest from Sofia Shinas and was then taking it to Brandon. What really happened? ***It would have saved Brandon's life had he was enforced to wear the vest but recall that it was the stunt coordinator of Brandon's when he voiced his opinion in the Book. Jeff Imada <u>stated it was crazy to consider a vest for a one-shot revolver.</u>*** Could it be Brandon was told or heard it was not needed for a one-shot revolver. Perhaps that was the reason. Questions to ponder:

"Why was it okay for a safety vest to be offered to Sofia Shinas for a gun scene that initially was said to be happening on that night, like she stated, yet, when change came in again and it was now Brandon Lee who was going to be shot then it was determined he didn't need a safety precaution or bullet-proof vest as with Shinas therefore, a bullet-proof vest had been offered and she had it in her possession for a while before it was taken from her and was not going to needed per Jeff Imada, to be offered to Brandon. Yes, to Sofia Shinas, and a No to Brandon."

Those are my thoughts. I did not read anyone questioning that point and so I have. The point of the matter is that a choice was made for Brandon from the very beginning (Jeff Imada) and I feel if Brandon would have known that danger was at foot and by taking risk not wearing the bullet-proof vest then perhaps, he wouldn't have been opposed to wearing it.

Stunt Coordinator Jeff Imada made his way to Brandon initially because he suspected "that's something catastrophic had happened." Really, he suspected something…perhaps it's because he knew in the back of his head a tiny obnoxious voice saying to him throughout the making of The Crow: *"He is going to die without a bulletproof vest."*

Obviously, it's stated in the book that Brandon himself chose not to wear one; nobody will ever know because we can't ask Brandon. We really can't ask him now, can we? And with his attitude towards not wearing a bullet-proof vest he didn't feel it coming, he didn't see it coming, the danger was not something he was worried about. And why would he not be worried? It's because of the ones he thought would have his back and took care of him, there was no rhyme or reason to worry that he could die. Jeff Imada made a misjudgment that took Brandon Lee's life at age 28, on the stage of Wilmington, North Carolina at Carolco Studios. As of today 30, years later nobody has stepped up and took responsibility for their actions that led to the death of a wonderful human being.

Actual Interview by Bobby Wygant on July 13, 1992, with Brandon Bruce Lee:

"Did you at any time use a stunt double?"

"Yeah, sure there's some going through a plate glass window, you know that's not me. I do all my own fighting because that's just part of the bag you know I mean it's part of why I am up on that film and I wouldn't want someone else to represent me my style in the film but stuff like going through a plate glass window or a getting thrown into a bar full of glass bottles Yeah I had a great stunt double named Jeff Cadiente. I've learned as I've gotten a little older that it just doesn't do anyone any good for you to get hurt on film because it just slows everything down, it costs everybody a lot of money and it puts a lot of people out of work. You know it's not a particularly responsible thing to do."

Some may believe it was the reckless part of who he was on his response to Sofia Shinas, (Shelly Webster). However, in my humble opinion; he didn't mean to put himself in the line of fire because it was a movie with dummy bullets with squibs and in *hindsight perhaps he put his trust on co-workers like DARRYLE LEVIN, BRUCE MERLIN AND DANIEL KUTTNER to keep him safe by providing what was meant not to kill him and why should he have worried that it could fail and kill him?*

Didn't Jeff Imada state he was safe? Were they not his friends, poor Brandon he didn't have a chance as he laid his trust on those who should have been thinking of his very life, a risk decision and Brandon died. The opposite of what Brandon had done for everyone's friends and co actors when he fought for better treatment and yet it was dismissed by the Producers as stated earlier. Brandon died a Hero! And that is my humble opinion. You are missed Brandon, and I am sorry that up until this book is penn I hope it does bring answers and I am hoping it continues to change the gun laws and regulations on any movie set and that is something I hope to see happen.

Lance Anderson says that he had constructed a special harness for Brandon some weeks before: *"I was under the impression that he wasn't gonna get shot, that he was gonna get stabbed. He's gonna get a knife thrown at him. And I built a harness to fit on the shoulder-the knife would be embedded in him, in the harness."*

When they were getting close to the scene, Anderson ran back to his trailer to get the harness and the fake knife. *"I showed it to Alex, and I said I gotta get this on him for the scene."* And he said, *"No, no, we've changed it. He's getting shot!"* But Lance also admits, *"I never received a script change deleting the knife from the scene."*

It's clear that during the making of the crow movie a lot of danger had surfaced, with accidents surfacing and time was of the essence and money was the huge talk about why safety precautions had not been handled in a manner to ensure the safety of all involved.

CHAPTER 9
Brandon almost going home

"Sheltering Sky" by Paul Bowles. *"Because you do not know when you will die, we get to think of life as being like an inexhaustible well. Yet everything happens only a certain number of times and a very small number really. How many more times will you remember a certain afternoon of your childhood, some afternoon that is so deeply a part of your being that you can't even conceive of your life without it? How many more times will you watch the full moon rise? Perhaps twenty. And yet it all seems limitless."* This exact quote was ENSCRIBED on Brandon's headstone which can be found in the Lake View Cemetery in Seattle, Washington state. Miramax proudly presents the very last interview with Brandon which includes exclusive never-before seen footage.

Brandon Lee had called his Momzo (mother) Linda Lee Cadwell on the night of his last workday. She stated: he was excited talking about his wedding plans with Eliza Hutton. I think of Brandon's contagious laughter, his beautiful smile, his intelligence, his appearance and ability to captivate anyone in an instant, his love for others, his respect for his comrades and his care of those he worked closely with and to his charm, to his light that shined brightly, and he was and is and should be the One and Only Eric Draven.

After 11:00 p.m. Brandon Lee walked onto the set ready for what would have been his last night at work on The Crow. Brandon was the main character as Eric Draven who was a rocker with long black hair in the movie script who was murdered by hoodlums along with his character's fiancée Shelly Webster who is played by Sofia Shinas.

However, on this night on set as Eric Draven the lead man Brandon Lee, he was wearing a velvet tight pair of pants, a leather jacket, a set of black laced boots and a T-shirt with Hangman's Joke', which was the name of his band (fictional band) for movie purposes, written across it.

As he walked past the trailer where he had spent hours getting ready for his final scene, Brandon felt a mix of emotions. He was excited to finish the movie that he had poured his heart and soul into, but also sad to leave behind the character that he had grown to love.

He had become Eric Draven, the tormented musician who rose from the dead to avenge his beloved Shelly. He had embodied the pain, the anger, and the passion of a man who had lost everything. Brandon had a special connection with The Crow, not only because it was his first leading role in a Hollywood production, but also because it was based on a comic book that he had admired since he was a teenager. He had read the graphic novel by James O'Barr, which was inspired by the author's own tragedy of losing his fiancée to a drunk driver.

Brandon had felt a kinship with O'Barr, who had used his art as a way of coping with his grief. Brandon had also experienced loss in his life, most notably the death of his father, the legendary martial artist and actor Bruce Lee, when Brandon was only eight years old.

Brandon had inherited his father's charisma, talent, and determination, but he had also struggled with living in his shadow. He had wanted to carve his own path in the film industry, and not be seen as a mere clone of his father.

He had rejected offers to star in martial arts movies that would have exploited his name and image, and instead chose projects that challenged him as an actor and allowed him to express his creativity.

He had taken acting classes, studied different genres and styles, and worked hard to improve his craft. He had also developed his own physical skills, combining his father's teachings with his own interests in boxing, fencing, and gymnastics.

The Crow was the perfect opportunity for Brandon to showcase his range and potential. He had impressed the director, Alex Proyas, with his audition, and had collaborated with him closely on developing the script, the look, and the tone of the movie. He had also formed a strong bond with the cast and crew, who had become like a family to him during the four months of filming in Wilmington, North Carolina.

He had especially enjoyed working with Sofia Shinas, who played his fiancée Shelly, and Michael Massee, who played Funboy, one of the thugs who killed them. He had also befriended the stunt coordinator, Jeff Imada, who had helped him design and execute the impressive fight scenes that showcased his agility and grace.

Brandon had put his soul into The Crow, and he was proud of the result. He knew that the movie would be a hit, and that it would launch his career to new heights. He had already signed on to star in two more films, Rapid Fire 2 and Dragon: The Bruce Lee Story, which would tell the story of his father's life.

He had also proposed to his girlfriend, Eliza Hutton, who was a story editor at Fox, and they had planned to get married in Mexico after he finished shooting The Crow. He was happy and optimistic about his future, and he couldn't wait to share his joy with the world.

But on that fateful night of March 31, 1993, Brandon's dream would be a dead end. As he walked onto the set of The Crow, ready to film his last scene, he had no idea that a tragic accident would end his life at the age of 28 and leave behind a legacy of sorrow and mystery. He got ready to leave his trailer and join the crew on the set. He put on his leather jacket and his makeup, which gave him the appearance of a pale and wounded avenger.

He grabbed his script and his sunglasses and headed out the door. He was eager to finish his role as Eric Draven, a rock musician who returns from the dead to avenge his murder and that of his fiancée. A negative event was approaching.

Rumors swirled. Was the bullet intentionally placed? The crew grappled with tragedy. Brandon's weight loss-40 pounds-was both physical and emotional. He sculpted himself into Eric Draven, the rock-and-roll spirit seeking vengeance. But the veil of silence remained.

Brandon's death echoed through the studio. Lind Lee Cadwell, his loving and supporting mother, now mourned her son. Shannon, his sister, lost her protector. The Key Players-the one's who held secrets, walked behind the scenes as the accident/death was being investigated by Detective Brian Pettus, they in fact escaped prosecution.

Laws on gun safety failed Brandon Bruce Lee. The Crow had claimed its own. As we turn the pages, we seek answers. Was it murder? Accident? The truth remains elusive. But awareness, like a beacon, guides us. Brandon light flickers in our memories, a legacy cut short. Brandon died a Hero as it Fade to black…

Nobody knew that fate would have other plans, and that The Crow would remain incomplete for several months after that night. Nobody knew that a tragic accident would end his life at the age of 28. Leave behind a legacy of sorrow and mystery.

Nobody knew that the gun that had been used prior and tested by Daniel Kuttner and Michael Massee was holding a fragment of a real bullet, which would fatally wound him when Michael Massee fired at him during the scene.

Nobody knew that he would collapse on the floor, bleeding profusely, and be rushed to the hospital, where he would undergo six hours of surgery before being pronounced dead.

Nobody knew that his mother, his sister, and his fiancée would receive the devastating news of his death, and that they would mourn him along with millions of fans around the world.

Nobody knew that his colleagues would be traumatized and heartbroken by the loss of their friend and collaborator, and that they would struggle to cope with the guilt and grief of witnessing his death.

Nobody knew that the director, who idolized Brandon and had gotten to know him before and after the filming, Alex Proyas would be shaken and would not want to finish the movie, but that he would be persuaded by Eliza Hutton and Linda Lee Cadwell, Brandon's mother, and Shannon Lee, his sister, to complete what Brandon had wanted to see done. And so he did.

Nobody knew that most of the cast would return and feel saddened to see Chad Stahelski, Brandon's stunt double, dressed up as Brandon Lee, and that it would be a painful thing to do to film without Brandon Lee.

And nobody would have known it was Chad Stahelski because the resemblance was daunting. He was agile and fit the script of Eric Draven so well that to see them both side by side would have confused even the best of cameras. And especially when Lance Anderson placed a cast mask on the two Chad Stahelski and Jeff Cadiente, and they looked identical if not exactly as Brandon Lee. However, after giving it much thought to finish the movie it was Chad Stahelski who was chosen to be Eric Draven scenes that Brandon didn't get to finish out.

Nobody knew that the movie would be released in 1994 and become a cult classic, and that Brandon's performance would be praised and celebrated as his best and final work.

Nobody knew that his death would spark a controversy and an investigation, and that it would raise questions about the safety and ethics of the film industry.

Nobody knew that his spirit would live on through his art and his legacy, and that he would be remembered as a talented and charismatic actor, a loving and generous person, and a son of a legend.

He had just finished talking to his mother, Linda Lee Cadwell, on the phone. He had told her that he was about to shoot the gun scene that night, and that it would be his last. He was happy to wrap up the filming and move on to his next projects. He had also shared with her his excitement about his upcoming wedding to Eliza, and how much he loved her. He ended the conversation by saying, "I love you, Momzo. Goodbye."

Brandon didn't know fate and the Crow had called his name: He hung up the phone and smiled. He felt a surge of gratitude and joy for everything he had in his life. He looked around his trailer and saw the pictures of his family and friends, his books and music, his martial arts equipment and memorabilia.

He felt a connection to his father Bruce Lee, who had inspired him to pursue his passion and follow his own path. He thought of his fans, who had supported him and appreciated his work. He thought of his colleagues, who had become his friends and collaborators.

He smiled knowing his colleagues had his back as they always had and even if fear struck him, he quickly shrugged it off because everyone had been looking forward to the ending of the filming in Wilmington, North Carolina and just like the rest he was happy it was his last night filming. He thought of his fiancée, who had been his soulmate and partner. He thought of his future, which was bright and promising.

He got up from his chair and put on his coat. He checked his hair and makeup in the mirror. He nodded to himself, satisfied with his look. He was ready to play Eric Draven, for the last time the character he had brought to life with his talent and charisma.

He grabbed his script and walked out of his trailer. He headed to the set, where the crew was waiting for him. He greeted them with a smile and a wave. He felt a rush of adrenaline and anticipation. He was eager to perform his last scene and give it his best. He didn't know that it would be his last scene ever.

What was going to transpire: "*Nobody Knew.*" Wearing his Hang Man's T-shirt, snug pants and black boots. He didn't know what had gone wrong and, in his head, he had to panic! (P.177) Lance was still surprised that: "He never bled…never bled. He looked like he was in shock. His eyes were open for a little while then they closed. And then he was just like, in shock. He was like, paralyzed. Just stiff. Not moving at all." He was shot and he never got back up. Hours later Brandon Bruce Lee was pronounced dead.

CHAPTER 10
Accident or Murdered?

In the Prologue, The Making of the Crow, The Story behind the film (P.5) The Property Master for over 28 years; Daniel Kuttner showed Michael Massee-the actor playing Funboy-that he had just loaded the .44 Magnum with which he would shoot Eric Draven, with a single, full blank charge, which would produce the desired flash of flame from the end of the barrel, for Alex Proyas the Director.

The cameras and sound began rolling. The First Assistant Director Steve Andrews, yelled "Action!" In the scene, we find Funboy, and his partner T-Bird played by David Patrick Kelly, during a violent assault on a pretty Brunette, Shelly Webster, Eric's fiancée. The front door opens, and Eric enters the Loft, carrying a bag of groceries. Funboy spins around, gun in hand, sees Eric and fires. The blank went off-Bang!

According to the book, the small explosive in the grocery bag detonated, exploding a milk container and ripping a hole in the bag. Eric grabbed his stomach, spun around and then sat to the ground against the doorway. Director Alex Proyas shouted, "CUT!"

The action stopped. Brandon never got back up!

Lance Anderson the Special Makeup Artist for Brandon Lee stated, "And he didn't get up, he just stayed there." Alex sat helplessly and in shock about what had happened, and nobody knew what or why Brandon just lay on the floor on that one last night of the filming of The Crow. Alex Proyas cried for his friend whom he loved so very much like a son.

He didn't know what had gone wrong and, in his head, he had to panic! (P.177) Lance was still surprised that: "He never bled…never bled. He looked like he was in shock. His eyes were open for a little while then they closed. And then he was just like, in shock. He was like, paralyzed. Just stiff. Not moving at all."

Brandon didn't know a real live bullet was waiting for him and would in fact take his life. "It is my opinion and evidence seem to speak for itself. Brandon was already dying once he was shot by what ballistics later stated was in fact a live .44 caliber bullet. It was repeated on live camera to be a live .44 caliber bullet that was lodged in Brandon's lower back on his body by Corner during the autopsy in Wilmington, North Carolina Police Department stated publicly.

Brandon's dying body was unconscious, and he never regained his consciousness as he succumbed to his injuries and as he had fallen hard against the only exit and doorway that leads outside of the studio. Greg Gale yelled, "Get the hell out of the way! Clear this area! Stay on the side!"

He was taking his last breath waiting for help to come his way while the Medic cut into his throat; "In order to give Brandon some chance of breathing. (P.178) Clyde Baisey had decided to give him a tracheotomy, closely watched by Darryl Levin, the same player who stated Brandon was at a safe place to be shot and that wearing a bulletproof vest was crazy."

Brandon was not shot in the throat. Baisey slips into his throat a device to intubate him which is running a tube in his lung. Did it investigate if Clyde Baisey had the right to cut into Brandon's throat and did anyone question his actions? While all this was going on Nini and Alex Proyas stayed as finally everyone left the set (30 left). Michelle Johnson was very concerned about Michael Massee, who by now had realized that something was wrong with the shot that he had fired, which appeared to have been the cause of Brandon's very serious injuries.

Robert Zuckerman heard, when Baisey finally made a pronouncement, "He just said, he has an abdominal wound, call 911. That's the first words that were said. That part I remember very clearly." Nothing could have saved Brandon and it's my opinion that Clyde Baisey knew that to be true, working on Brandon was not appropriate. He was already dead, no pulse, flat lining and he did not regain his consciousness."

When Clyde played medic on him, the body was already going through the process of what happens when a human body dies and it's the opposite of being alive it begins to shut down all the internal organs, the brain as we know goes last and its why nothing the doctors tried on him before and after surgery saved Brandon from dying, my thoughts, my opinion after reading and researching Brandon's death.

Baisey said, "Get an ambulance here, now and clear the set."

Arriane Phillips saw that: Alex Proyas just kind of slumped on the floor. Everyone had gone out of the room, and Alex had just kind of slumped on the floor, and Nini, the Script Supervisor, had slumped next to him, with her arm around him, and I was in shock."

Clyde (P.179) Baisey observed that "Brandon's condition had not improved. He had no pulse to this point and that is very serious. Brandon had not recovered consciousness at all." He couldn't have if he was already dead.

The conversation that Clyde Baisey had with the medics upon arrival goes as follows: "Baisey explained, "Go ahead and set a couple of IV lines. I'll get him intubated, which is running a tube in his lung. I said, "We can hook him directly to an air control system and you can go ahead and give him one hundred percent oxygen."

Clyde Baisey had hooked up a heart monitor on Brandon. They saw the flat line twice. Clyde Baisey continued to explain that he initially displayed what is called EMD, which is electromechanical dissociation, or now it is referred to as pulseless electrical activity, PEA. Which means that the brain is sending electrical impulses to the heart muscle, but because there is no blood circulating in the system, the heart is unable to beat. In his words, "the last three things that die on a body is the heart, the brain and the lungs." (P.180)

In the ambulance despite 6 IVs, pumping into Brandon the fluids because of the blood loss internally, they could not feel no heartbeat, despite the monitors showing that he had a normal heart rate.

According to the same article, Brandon Lee was rushed to the New Hanover Regional Medical Center in Wilmington, North Carolina. N.C, profusely hemorrhaging. After an X-ray it was determined that some kind of object had lodged itself against his spine, though no one had any idea what that object was. Lee was taken to emergency surgery where doctors attempted to repair the damage to his internal organs. The bullet had severed a major artery, and his blood wouldn't clot. He was pronounced dead at 1:03 PM on March 31, 1993, some 12 hours after.

Jeff Imada had returned to the set as soon as the ambulance had left the studio for the hospital, and said, "I got together with the prop guy and the effects guy and tried to figure out if anything else went wrong." (P.182)

According to Greg Gale, Associate Producer, "They looked around and investigated the bag and everything. Jeff Imada, Stunt Coordinator, looked at the video recorder by the main camera over Masse's shoulder, onto Brandon. (P.182) One thing he had looked for was where Masse had aimed the gun.

To Imada, "It didn't, like it was aimed directly at him. It didn't seem like it was intentional, like and aimed directly at the door, it was more like a waver across, and he got shot. Because he was playing like he was high or drunk or whatever."

(P.182) "Even if was using the gun with a blank in it and aimed it at him he was more than a safe distance away. It's very safe. As far as distance-wise, for the blank." After he had looked at the video, Jeff Imada says that "They took the videotape and the film footage and took it away to lock it up."

Again, in my opinion just like any other scene in real life dealing with an accident, why did the crew members go back and look at what may have happened to Brandon? It's not their job description and it belongs to real professionals who do their job daily for critical death and accident scenes. Yet, the crew went back to look. To put away evidence. Really? I wasn't aware that at any murder, death or accident scene anyone could leave without the police giving them permission.

"Somebody really screwed up. At some point, somebody must take responsibility, even if it's just in their heart," says co-star, actor Ernie Hudson. (P.132) Hudson could not understand why the production would take huge chances in losing their star by putting him at such risk. Ernie Hudson was upset that a lot of what he saw was about the money and nobody wanted to come out and say it. It was about the money! Guess what? A box of dummy rounds would have cost $20 dollars!

It was determined by the Wilmington Police to be an accidental death and no criminal charges were filed. It remains as such today after 30 years of Brandon Lee's death. I'm impressed and thankful for the article that I used to bring forth the thoughts and words of "He shined brilliantly and needs to be remembered." Budomate.

According to the writings on "The Crow" The Story behind the film by Bridget Baiss, (P.183), it was only Daniel Kuttner, Bruce Merlin, Greg Gale, Robert Zuckerman, and Jeff Imada who were involved in the initial attempts to see what happened and preserve the scene and the film.

CHAPTER 11
Daunting

What began to run in my mind was the scenario before the death of Brandon Lee, was an unimaginable story told by Most. (P.158) Producer Jeff Most was sitting in his office that evening as Brandon walked past on his way to work. (10ish perhaps?) Jeff was on the phone, but he saw Brandon through his glass office window. "He waved to me," says Most.

He was all dressed in white, almost like an Indian white, a hundred percent cotton shirt. Nothing he was wearing as a character costume. He waved and it had a different connotation of a wave than expected. And I waved back at Brandon, and I said to the person on the phone, 'that's strange", he waved at me like he's saying goodbye. Maybe he forgot, he's shooting for "two more days."

That was just an offhand comment, but I just remember reflecting on it, because there was something, maybe the mind plays tricks, and your last memory is something different than how it went down, but there was an ethereal quality to that wave, and my seeing him that last time."

Was it Brandon who waved at producer Most? Or was it someone else? Or a double stunt? A premonition? A farewell? A coincidence? No one can say for sure, but most will always remember that moment as the last time he saw his friend and colleague alive. I know it sounds like a crazy conspiracy about this.

He never made it back home alive. He never got married to his love. He was shot in a tragic accident on the set of The Crow, a film that was supposed to be his breakthrough role. The bullet that struck him was lodged in his spine, and despite the efforts of the paramedics and surgeons, he could not be saved. He was pronounced dead at 1:03 a.m. on March 31, 1993, at the age of 28.

The film's director, Alex Proyas, decided to complete the film as a tribute to Lee, using body doubles and digital effects to fill in the scenes that he had not finished. The Crow was released in 1994 and became a cult classic, but also a haunting reminder of the potential dangers of filmmaking and the need for stricter safety measures. *The Making of Shadows*:

In the hallowed halls of Hollywood, where secrets and spotlights intertwine, a tragedy unfolded-a tale of shadows and silence. Brandon Bruce Lee, son of the legendary Bruce Lee, had stepped onto the set of The Crow one last time, a film that would etch his name into cinematic history. But had other plans. *A Veil of Silence:*

"Truth is the medicine some can't handle", they say. And so, *it was-the truth veiled*, whispers stifled. *The Key Players*-the architects of fate-held their secrets close. They danced on the edge of risk, indifferent to the abyss yawning beneath their actions. *Bridget Bais's book, "The Making of The Crow,"* peeled back layers-the script, the makeup, the set. Page by page, it revealed the dance between life and art, between *Brandon and Eric Draven an excellent art of words per the writer*. But some truths remain elusive, like shadows slipping through fingers.

Echoes of a Sacrifice: March 31, 1993-a night etched in sorrow. Brandon, the rock star turned phantom, wore the black leather jacket, the tight corduroys. His hair, once wild, now framed a face painted pale. He shed 40 pounds, not just for the role, but as an offering-an act of devotion. The Key Players moved in shadows. Their choices, their indifference-it led to tragedy. Brandon's last breath echoed through the Carolco Studios. Lind Lee Cadwell, his Momzo, clung to memories. Stabbing her inner spirit just like daggers where there could be no comfort or peace, her only son had been taken away and it left her in a pool of tears that would prove to become endless. Written in the book was the saddened truth on page 190 after the surgery was complete, the doctor gave an update. At about 4 a.m., someone from the production office called Brandon's mother Linda Lee Cadwell, in Boise Idaho. Until that point Brandon's mother, had not been told of the seriousness of Brandon's injury. Now the news was that Brandon had gotten out of surgery and that the doctors were able to stop the bleeding and had repaired his aorta. The Production Office had told Lind that she, and Brandon's sister Shannon, should come to North Carolina immediately.

In between the sheets of this book are words that can never be ripped apart to create a story of laughter that could have brought a smile to your face if *he had never died* and instead, we would be saturated with just listening to Brandon Bruce Lee laugh endlessly. Salty tears flow like the ocean waves infinitely. Until we meet again Brandon Bruce Lee. Fly high free like the Raven.

CHAPTER 12
KEY PLAYERS

1. JEFF IMADA, STUNT COORDINATOR

2. JEFF IMADA, FIGHT CHOREOGRAPHY

3. JEFF CADIENTE, STUNT DOUBLE

4. CHAD STAHELSKI, STUNT DOUBLE

5. ALEX PROYAS, DIRECTOR

6. JAMES O'BARR WRITER, GRAPHIC NOVEL

7. DAVID J. SHOW, SCREENWRITER

8. EDWARD PRESSMAN, PRODUCER

9. JEFF MOST, PRODUCER (HIRED BY PRESSMAN) (P.251)

10. ROBERT L. ROSEN, (BOB) EXECUTIVE PRODUCER

11. ARIANNE PHILLIPS, COSTUME DESIGNER

12. GREGORY A. GALE, ASSOCIATE PRODUCER

13. MARTHE PINEAU, SET DECORATOR

14. ROBERT ZUCKERMAN, STILL PHOTOGRAPHER

15. LANCE ANDERSON, SPECIAL MAKE-UP EFFECTS

16. DANIEL KUTTNER, PROPMASTER

17. CHARLENE HAMER, ASSISTANT PROP MASTER

18. JIM MOYER, WEAPONS SPECIALIST

19. CLYDE BAISEY, MEDIC

20. DARRLY LEVIN, WARDROBE SUPERVISOR

21. BRUCE MERLIN, SPECIAL EFFECTS TECHNICIAN

22. GRANT HILL, ASSOCIATE PRODUCER/PRODUCTION

CHAPTER 12
Inequity

"THING ABOUT POLICE WORK, YOU DON'T ASK QUESTIONS, YOU DON'T KNOW THE ANSWERS TO." (P.203)

Why did the Officer get offered the job to handle the case if he had no knowledge about the movie industry? He admitted that he didn't even know Brandon Lee. Could he have overlooked anything while he investigated and allowed criminals to be set free to live their lives while Brandon was now placed in a compartment in the ground at the Lake View Cemetery, in Seattle, Washington? 30 years now to be exact! And yet so many questions were left unanswered. Why?

The bullet had entered Brandons front abdomen, just below his belly button had the power to easily rip through all the organs and cut directly through the center of the fork of the artery. Then it hit his spine and stopped. In fact, he had been hit in an extraordinary critical spot. At the back of the body, near the lower spine, the major artery forks, to supply blood to each leg. (P.188) In his investigations Detective Brian Pettus had immediately deduced that a bullet was fired into Brandon from the .44 Magnum.

(P.184) According to the police investigations by Pettus, it was Daniel Kuttner, Bruce Merlin, Greg Gale, Jeff Imada, and Robert Zuckerman were involved in these initial attempts to see what had happened, and to preserve the scene and film, meaning and further known that (P.182-183)

Jeff Imada says, "They took the videotape and the film footage and took it away, to lock it up."

However, the report also stated that the dummy bullets were made by the crew themselves and removing the gunpowder from live rounds, which was a violation of the safety protocols and the studio's policies.

The crew claimed that they did this because they could not find any commercially available dummy bullets in the local stores, but this was later proven to be false by the police. Because a box of dummy rounds would have cost the crew and film industry $20. It's noted that the pawn shop stated that they would have had the dummy rounds available maybe as late as one day, but they would have done it and it may have been what may have stopped the death from happening that later was called "accidental." The crew admitted that they did not check the weapons properly before each scene and that they did not have a qualified armor on the set.

THE CROWVISION (P.205-208) GUNS, AMMO, BLANKS, DISMANTLING, DEATH

"ALL WERE SAVING THEIR OWN BUTTS. IF THEY HAD ADMITTED FAULT THAT WOULD BE CHARGED FOR A MURDER. THEY WERE SCROUNGING, TRYING TO SAVE THEIR OWN CAREERS, ALREADY THE MOVIE HAD NUMEROUS MISHAPS AND NOW A DEATH OF BRANDON LEE."-Detective Brian Pettus.

According to R. E. Payne the following. Excerpts from Part-3

Brandon's mother Linda Lee Cadwell, on behalf of the Estate of Brandon Lee, filed a civil suit almost immediately. We obtained a copy of the suit which was later permanently sealed at the request of Caldwell's attorneys. "We spoke with several law enforcement officials, including the local district attorney's office, and they all agreed that it as Cadwell's quick acceptance to settle the civil suit, that douse the flames of investigators to investigate the death as diligently as they would any other that did not involve Hollywood.

"The settlement stopped the investigation immediately, Officially, the case was closed." "The agreement, obtained by our investigators from sources in Wilmington, is a remarkable tribute to an excellent lawyer on behalf of Cadwell. There is something in it for everyone, especially, of course Linda Lee Cadwell, the beneficiary of the largesse of the insurance companies, and even the 14 defendants named in her suit! "The 14 could walk without further exposure and without having to admit any wrongdoing." The Video Tape of the Shooting of Brandon Lee.

"For a price, local sources knowledgeable about the case, offered to let me view the tape (used to video each scene filmed). Take notes, but do not copy it. I agreed to meet them in the parking lot of the Holiday Inn at Wrightsville Beach. The hotel was closed for renovations.

They had been told we were in my Cadillac with Louisiana plates. They said they were driving a van, with no plates. "They were."

Excerpts from Part-4

"We located another firearms expert who tested the 'official' theory. He took a .44 Magnum like the one used by Michael Massee that killed Brandon Lee. He lodged a dummy bullet in the barrel and then loaded a full load blank. Firing into a sack of sand placed 20 feet away (the approximate distance between Brandon Lee and Massee), the bullet traveled only four feet before falling harmlessly to the ground."

Unsolved Mysteries Part 1

According to the Detective Rodney Simmons and Brian Pettus stated in "Unsolved Mysteries" Part 1. "They were filming a pawn shop scene, and they needed items from a local pawn shop in Wilmington. They gathered over 100 props and among them was a box of live .44 magnum bullets.

Unsolved Mysteries Continuation Part 2:

A strange journey of bullets after about 5-6 months we knew pretty much where the Gun had gone, who had handled the bullets, who had handled the gun and at what level of responsibility everybody was.

Everything was at last ready for the cast and crew to rehearse the scene. (P.168) Funboy the character that Michael Masse would play and point and shoot the revolver at Brandon and it was a .44 Magnum with a white handle, (P.167) but that it would be very loud. Alex Proyas chose Massee as the shooter. (P.165)

"But I'm also gonna say that these guys from Imada and Brandon, and even our Effects guy, were not new at what they were doing. They looked at this and they prepared people the way they should've been prepared. We didn't put bullet-proof vests on people for revolvers being shot.

"Darryl Levin, Wardrobe Supervisor" with Jeff Imada backing him up on this idea of not using a bullet-proof vest for a revolver scene that Brandon was going to be shot from…Darryl Levin was insistent on this point and repeated it many times: "No, we never did that kinda stuff. Bulletproof vest? Excuse me. (P.161-162) What are you? Crazy?"

GENTLEMEN! BB GUNS CAN KILL.

Darryl Levin, Wardrobe Supervisor, AND Jeff Imada Stunt Coordinator (Brandon's friend for years practicing choreography at Brandon's own backyard.) Question is? Was it Crazy? Ask yourselves who died in all of this? Jeff Imada? Or Darrly Levine? Or Brandon Lee?

"The only time you ever use that protection, is if somebody in a shot comes up to you with a full-point blank, because a blank with powder can still affect you-then we put on a bullet-proof vest. We were halfway across the room. There was no reason. We would not have done that. That would not have been in the cards."

The stunt coordinator agrees with Levine that a vest was totally unnecessary in this scene. "It was in a bag pointing away from him…Brandon was more than the required distance from the gun" It's your words. Why am I asking? Were you correct in your line of thinking? Did you save a life? Or did life get distinguished?

What about the purchasing of a License to purchase Live Bullets? Who was in CHARGE? DID THEY DO A GOOD JOB? What protocol on buying ammunition or ammo followed through? Did the Wilmington, North Carolina Police do the investigation? Yes, they did. You will see it on the same video, I was saddened.

Yet, blown away by the writings of R.E. Payne.

Question: Did Brandon Lee get any information about the said mix up for the bullets and then dismantled by the prop crew? Answer is no, he did not! Do you know why? (P.205) Well, a couple of weeks ago nobody could give us the time, exact date that they found them, and nobody could give us the exact date they had made them. (Prop people) Think about that. Do you see the questions? And why did nobody dare give time, dates and resist doing so? (P.205-207) And

Detective Brian Pettus' sources would not go on the record. He says they were: The guys that know what's going on. The workers know what's going on. They didn't wanna go on record, because it was their butts if they got caught telling us. But they were coming forth and telling us these things.

Further it was stated in the same pages of the book that if they had come forward with the TRUTH and not hide behind their own words. You all knew this. You were his friends, and you should have had his back. But did you? Was his best interest at heart? You knew what you had all done from the time you chose to dismantle the bullets you were all aware of the risk that would and could cause bodily harm? You all acted with intent to choose it? After you heard of Brandon's death you became indifferent to the risk. The reason why you chose it and caused bodily harm. You failed Brandon Lee and his entire Lee family. See?

Therefore, it is possible that some of the crew members tampered with the evidence after the shooting to cover up their mistakes or to hide something more sinister. However, the police did not find any conclusive proof of intentional homicide and ruled the death as accidental.

The case was closed without any criminal charges, but the Lee family filed a civil lawsuit against the studio and the crew, which was settled out of court for an undisclosed amount.

I don't believe it was an accident waiting to happen. Did he lose his career? Yes, he did. Did he lose the opportunity to spend time with his family? Yes, he did. And now you know my reason for studying and writing this book. Hopefully you will get something out of it and come to your own conclusion on the alleged accident.

Knowing how much of a loss it was for the Lee family. I think of him in this way even if I never got to meet him, and it's with my own desire to Penn a book written about Brandon and offering some kind of closure to others like me who continued to ask why and how it all happened. To point them out. I thank you all who read this.

The near future in a Promised Paradise (Revelation 21;3,4) Rest in Peace to the "Light that Shined So Brightly" that was distinguished forevermore.

"They have not listened yet, Brandon; but perhaps they will. You Will Never Be Forgotten, Brandon Bruce Lee."

(Cited from Movieweb.com)

We're remembering Brandon Lee on the 31st anniversary of his passing. Son of the legendary martial artist and actor Bruce Lee, Brandon is perhaps best known for his leading role in Alex Proyas' The Crow. The cult classic was released posthumously after Brandon was killed in a tragic accident on the set of the movie, forever marking March 31 as a dark day for the Lee family and all of his fans. Each year on the anniversary of his death, his family shares a tribute to him: "31 years gone today but we feel you with us still. Love you, Bran thanks for surrounding us with your love always" Shannon Lee

TO BRANDON FROM ROBERT ZUCKERMAN:

And he has left us,

Yet in his absence,

His presence is

And shall be

Stronger than ever,

For he is

everywhere now,

and he is

inside of us.

We who witnessed

The brilliance

Of his flame

And were warned

by its heat;

We, who heard

The chimes

Of his churchbell laughter

Ring the plains

of starry dawns,

We, who stand.

in the pure rain

of his divine

And noble spirit

Are now its

blessed, honored keepers.

Within and through us

He shall live on

And our lives

Shall ever be enriched

by him

In ways

wonderous and untold

Fly high, dear friend.

(P.196-197)

THE END